# SMART W

## READER

# REPTILES
## and
# AMPHIBIANS

Christine A. Caputo

SCHOLASTIC INC.

# What are SMART WORDS?

Smart Words are frequently used words that are critical to understanding concepts taught in the classroom. The more Smart Words a child knows, the more easily he or she will grasp important curriculum concepts. Smart Words Readers introduce these key words in a fun and motivational format while developing important literacy skills. Each new word is highlighted, defined in context, and reviewed. Engaging activities at the end of each chapter allow readers to practice the words they have learned.

**ISBN** 978-0-545-46701-8

**Packaged by Q2A Bill Smith**

Copyright © 2012 by Scholastic Inc.

**Picture Credit:** t= top, b= bottom, l= left, r= right, c= center

Cover Page: Leungchopan/Shutterstock.
Title Page: David Gartland/Fotolia.
Contents Page: Julija Sapic/Shutterstock.

4: Peter Leahy/Shutterstock; 5: Vadim Petrakov/Shutterstock; 6: Vladj55/Shutterstock; 7: Ryan M. Bolton/Shutterstock; 8tl: Mighty Sequoia Studio/Shutterstock; 8tr: Susan Flashman/Shutterstock; 8bl: Nodff/Shutterstock; 8bc: Karel Gallas/Shutterstock; 8br: Chris2766/Shutterstock; 9tl: Matt Jeppson/Shutterstock; 9tr: Willie Davis/Shutterstock; 9b: Julian W/Shutterstock; 10: WitthayaP/Shutterstock; 11:Chris Mattison/Frank Lane Picture Agency/Corbis; 12: Fritz Rauschenbach/Corbis; 13t: AlessandroZocc/ Shutterstock; 13b: Cynthia Kidwell/Shutterstock; 16: Matt Jeppson/Shutterstock; 17: Jason Patrick Ross/Shutterstock; 18cl: Dirk Ercken/Shutterstock; 18cr: Matt Jeppson/ Shutterstock; 19tl: Joe Farah/Shutterstock; 19tr: John A. Anderson/Shutterstock; 19b: Michael & Patricia Fogden/Corbis; 20: Cosmin Manci/Shutterstock; 21t: Formiktopus/ Shutterstock; 21b: Scott Leigh/Istockphoto; 22: Robin Winkelman/Dreamstime; 23: worldswildlifewonders/Shutterstock; 24: Dr. Michael R. Loomis, DVM North Carolina Zoological Park; 25: kgb224/Shutterstock; 26c: Designpics/123RF; 26b: Roberta Olenick/All Canada Photos/Corbis; Chris Mattison/Frank Lane Picture Agency/Corbis; Wayne Lynch/All Canada Photos/Corbis; 28: Melinda Fawver/Shutterstock; 29: Pius Lee/Shutterstock.

Q2A Bill Smith Art Bank: 14-15.

12 11 10 9 8 7 6 5 4 3 2 1          12 13 14 15 16 17/0

Printed in the U.S.A.
First printing, September 2012

40

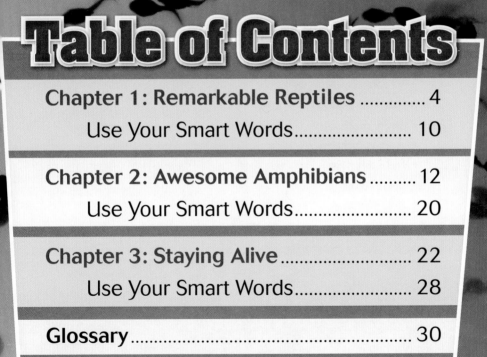

# Table of Contents

# Chapter 1

# Remarkable Reptiles

A big green lizard. A small black turtle. A long striped snake. What do these animals have in common? They are all reptiles! Reptiles all share some specific characteristics, or traits. Let's find out more about these traits!

## How to Spot a Reptile

**Look for these traits:**

- has a backbone
- is an ectotherm
- has scaly skin
- most lay eggs
- breathes air

Sea turtles are reptiles. They have shells attached to their backbones and they swim to the surface to breathe.

An animal with a backbone is a **vertebrate**. A backbone is made up of individual bones. The bones are attached to one another in a way that allows the backbone to bend as the animal moves. All reptiles have backbones.

What else do all reptiles have in common? They all breathe air, which contains oxygen. Even reptiles that spend most of their time under water come up to the surface to breathe air.

**Temperature** is a measure of how hot or cold something is. Animals whose body temperature depends on their surroundings are **ectotherms**. All reptiles are ectotherms.

Lying out in the sunlight is one way reptiles like this iguana get warm. They slip back into the shade to cool off.

## SMART WORDS

**reptile** an animal that has a backbone, breathes air, has scaly skin, depends on its surroundings to maintain its body temperature, and may lay eggs or give live birth

**vertebrate** an animal with a backbone

**temperature** a measure of how hot or cold something is

**ectotherm** an animal whose body temperature depends on its surroundings

# Living on Land

If you look at a snake from far away, you might think it would feel slimy. If you touch it, you would find out that it is actually quite dry. Snakes and most other reptiles have tough, dry skin covered by pointy **scales**. Scales are thin, flat, overlapping pieces of hard skin that prevent the skin from drying out. They also help protect the reptile from harm and sometimes help it blend into its surroundings to hide from other animals.

Reptile scales, like the ones on this python, contain the same substance as your fingernails!

A few types of reptiles, such as skinks and boa constrictors, have live babies, but most lay **eggs** to produce young. An egg contains the young reptile along with the food it needs as it develops. When it is ready to live on its own, the young reptile breaks out of the egg.

The outside, or shell, of the egg protects the young reptile from the outside environment. It also keeps in water to prevent the young reptile from drying out on land. Most reptile eggs have a soft shell that can bend. That's because reptiles often drop their eggs in holes or place them under rocks. If the shells were hard, they might crack!

The spiny softshell turtle grows inside the egg for about 55 to 60 days.

SMART WORDS

**scales** thin, flat, overlapping pieces of hard skin that cover the bodies of most reptiles

**egg** an oval or round structure that holds a young animal and the food it needs to develop

# Kinds of Reptiles

Scientists **classify** the many types of reptiles into groups based on how they are alike and different. There are four main groups of reptiles.

## Alligator and Crocodile

| Alligator | Crocodile |
|---|---|
| long, strong body | long, strong body |
| 4 legs, long tail | 4 legs, long tail |
| wide, U-shaped mouth | pointed, V-shaped mouth |
| 4th tooth on lower jaw sticks out of mouth | 4th tooth on lower jaw is covered when mouth is closed |
| lives in freshwater | lives in salt water |

## Turtle, Tortoise, and Terrapin

| Turtle | Tortoise | Terrapin |
|---|---|---|
| shell on the back | shell on the back | shell on the back |
| webbed feet or flippers | round, stumpy feet | webbed feet with claws |
| lives mostly in water | lives on land | lives on land near water |
| mostly swims, sometimes walks | walks | swims and walks |

## Lizard and Snake

| Lizard | Snake |
|---|---|
| long body and tail | long body and tail |
| wide jaws | wide jaws |
| uses tongue for smelling | uses tongue for smelling |
| most have 4 legs | no legs |
| sheds skin in patches | sheds skin in one piece |

## Tuatara

| | |
|---|---|
| only live on islands near New Zealand | hunt at night, sleep during the day |
| spikes on back | live in holes in the ground |

Tuataras keep growing, but very slowly, for the first 35 years of their lives. They can live to be up to 100 years old!

## SMART WORD

**classify** to arrange animals into groups according to how they are alike and different

9

Match each description to the correct
Smart Word.

| reptile | vertebrate | temperature |
| ectotherm | scales | egg | classify |

1. a measure of how hot or cold something is

2. an animal that has a backbone, breathes air, has scaly skin, depends on its surroundings to maintain its body temperature, and lays eggs or has live babies

3. an oval or round structure that holds a young animal and the food it needs to develop

4. to group animals according to how they are alike and different

5. any animal with a backbone

6. an animal whose body temperature depends on its surroundings

7. thin, flat, overlapping pieces of hard skin that cover the bodies of most reptiles

Answers on page 32

# Talk Like a Scientist

An exhibit at a nature preserve displays a lizard, an alligator, and a turtle. Use your Smart Words to write a sign to describe the traits of each of these reptiles.

# SMART FACTS

## Did You Know?

Pythons kill their food by squeezing it. They coil around another animal until it can't breathe anymore. Then they eat it.

## That's Amazing!

Pythons can swallow animals that are much bigger than they are. Their jaws actually come apart so they can stretch their mouths around the food.

## Protective Mothers

Python mothers lay their eggs and then coil around them to keep them safe and warm. Once the eggs hatch, the mother leaves the babies to survive on their own.

# Chapter 2

# Awesome Amphibians

Splash! A giant frog leaps into a pond. It looks slimy and lives near water, just like a reptile. But is it a reptile? No! A frog is an **amphibian**. Amphibians share some traits with reptiles. They have other traits that make them very different from reptiles. Let's find out more about these traits!

## How to Spot an Amphibian

**Look for these traits:**
- has a backbone
- is an ectotherm
- most have smooth skin
- lives part of its life in water
- depends on water to produce young

Frogs live near fresh water on every continent except Antarctica. No frogs live there!

The name *amphibian* comes from a Greek word that means "double life." That's because most amphibians spend part of their lives on land and part in water. Usually, young amphibians spend their first few months or years in water. As they get older, they move onto land.

Fire salamanders live in parts of Europe, northern Africa, and the Middle East. They stay in the shade near ponds and streams.

Panamanian golden frogs live in high mountain forests of Panama. They stay close to the streams that flow through the forests.

SMART WORD

**amphibian** an ectothermic vertebrate that lays eggs in water and usually has smooth, slimy skin

# Changing Over Time

As part of their double lives, amphibians change as they grow. All of the changes that an animal goes through from the time it is born until it can produce young is known as its **life cycle**. Part of the life cycle for most amphibians is known as **metamorphosis**. As shown in the diagram, the body of a frog changes a lot during this time.

Frogs lay eggs in water. They often look like a pile of jelly. Some frogs lay thousands of eggs at once.

After about four months, the froglet becomes an adult frog that can live on land. When it is time for the frog to produce young, it goes back to the water to lay eggs and the cycle begins again.

For most kinds of frogs, it takes from a few days to a few weeks for a tadpole to form. When it's ready, the tadpole breaks out of the egg.

The tail forms as the young tadpole grows.

In a month or two, the tadpole forms legs and becomes known as a froglet. The back legs grow before the front legs.

After about three months, the tail shrinks and the back legs grow.

## SMART WORD

**life cycle** the changes an animal goes through from the time it is born until it can produce young

**metamorphosis** part of the life cycle during which an animal's body changes in form

# Living Near Water

You breathe through your nose and mouth, but guess how amphibians breathe – through their skin! Amphibians have thin, **moist**, or slightly wet, skin. Oxygen from the air can pass right through an amphibian's skin. Water can also pass through the skin. So, in a way, amphibians can drink through their skin, too!

When amphibians are young and live in water, their skin is not out in the air. They need another way to breathe. In water, they use structures called **gills** to breathe. Gills are like filters on the sides of their bodies. When water moves across an amphibian's gills, oxygen moves from the water into the amphibian's body.

gills

The grotto salamander lives in deep, dark caves. For the first two or three years of its life, the grotto salamander has gills. Once it becomes an adult, the gills disappear.

The spotted salamander lives under rocks or logs near water to keep its skin moist.

Once they live on land, amphibians use structures called **lungs** to breathe. Lungs are like balloons that can fill with air. When air moves into the lungs, oxygen moves from the air into the amphibian's body.

Amphibians are usually as slimy as they look. That's because their skin makes a gooey substance known as mucus. This clear liquid helps protect the amphibian's skin. It also helps more oxygen pass through the skin into the body.

## SMART WORDS

**moist** damp or slightly wet

**gills** body structures that act like filters to move oxygen from the water into the body of an animal living in the water

**lungs** balloon-like structures that move oxygen from the air into the bodies of most animals that live on land

# Kinds of Amphibians

Scientists have discovered more than 6,000 different types of amphibians! Each type of amphibian is known as a **species**. All of the animals of the same species are very similar and can produce young with the same traits. Scientists classify the many different species into three main groups.

## Frog and Toad

| Frog | Toad |
|---|---|
| no tail as an adult | no tail as an adult |
| usually has smooth, moist skin | usually has warty, dry skin |
| needs to live near water | does not need to live near water |
| long back legs | short back legs |
| moves in big jumps | moves in short hops |

## SMART WORDS

**species** the most specific grouping of animals that share similar traits and can produce young

**burrow** to dig a hole or tunnel into the soil

# Salamander and Newt

| Salamander | Newt |
| --- | --- |
| long tail | long tail |
| 4 legs | 4 legs |
| walks and swims | walks and swims |
| smooth, slick skin | dry, warty skin |
| lives mostly in water | lives mostly on land |

## Caecilian

| live in warm, wet areas | look like big worms |
| --- | --- |
| no legs or tail | burrow into soil |

Caecilians have hard, thick, pointy skulls that help them burrow into soil.

Answer each question with a Smart Word.

| amphibian | life cycle | metamorphosis |
| moist | gills | lungs | species | burrow |

1. What are structures that amphibians use to breathe on land when they don't use their skin?

2. What is the process through which the body of an amphibian changes in form?

3. What does an amphibian do when it digs a hole or tunnel in the soil?

4. What are structures that amphibians use to take oxygen from water?

5. What term describes a group of organisms that have similar traits and can produce young?

6. What term describes an animal that is an ectothermic vertebrate that spends part of its life in water and part on land?

7. What word describes something that is damp or slightly wet?

8. What is the process of changes in an animal from the time it is born until it can produce young?

Answers on page 32

# Talk Like a Scientist

Use your Smart Words to explain how an amphibian is different from a reptile.

# SMART FACTS

## How Colorful!

When an animal swoops in to feed on this frog, it pops open its bright red eyes and scares the animal away.

## That's Amazing!

A female red-eyed tree frog lays her eggs on leaves that hang over ponds. When the tadpoles hatch from the eggs, they fall right into the water!

## Did You Know?

Once they grow from tadpoles into frogs, tree frogs climb up nearby branches to live in the trees. They have suction cups on their fingers and toes to help them climb.

# Chapter 3

# Staying Alive

You wouldn't find a turtle living in Antarctica because it would get too cold. You wouldn't find a caecilian living in a tree because it burrows underground. Every kind of animal lives in a special habitat.

Each species makes **adaptations**, or changes, that help it survive in its special habitat. Skin color and covering (such as scales), or body parts (such as sharp teeth), can be adaptations. The way an animal behaves, such as hiding in small places, can also be an adaptation.

The black mamba is one of the most feared snakes in Africa. It has enough venom in one bite to kill over 20 people.

One adaptation that many reptiles and amphibians have is poison, or **venom**. Many venomous animals have bright colors on their bodies. These colors often warn **predators** to stay away. A predator is an animal that hunts and eats another animal for food. Any animal that is hunted and eaten for food by another animal is known as **prey**.

The poison dart frog got its name because the native people of South America used the frog's poison to coat the tips of blow darts. They used the darts to hunt for small animals.

## SMART WORDS

**adaptation** a change that an animal goes through so it survives better in its habitat

**venom** poison produced by an animal

**predator** an animal that hunts and eats other animals for food

**prey** an animal that is hunted and eaten by other animals

# Safe and Sound

Have you ever played hide-and-seek? If so, you know the best way to avoid being caught is to find a good hiding spot. Another is to blend into your surroundings so you can't be seen.

Animals often hide from predators in the same ways. Many reptiles and amphibians have skin colors that help them blend into their surroundings to make them hard to see. This adaptation is known as **camouflage**.

The Cameroon toad looks like a fallen tree leaf.
A predator might not spot this toad as it passes by.

Even if a predator catches some kinds of reptiles or amphibians, the prey can still get away. A predator might think it has found a quick meal when it grabs on to a gecko's tail, but the gecko has a surprise. It can drop part of its tail right off! As the predator watches or wrestles with the wiggling tail, the gecko runs away. It will regrow a new tail part over the next few weeks.

Dropping its tail off can help keep the gecko alive!

## SMART WORD

**camouflage** the ability of an animal to blend into its surroundings because of its coloring

# Surviving Harsh Weather

What do you do when the weather is too cold or too hot? Do you put on a coat or turn on a fan? Because reptiles and amphibians are ectotherms, or animals whose body temperature depends on their surroundings, staying out in extreme heat or cold can be dangerous — or even deadly! These animals take action to survive when the weather isn't just right.

In the cold of winter, many reptiles and amphibians burrow deep in the ground or slither into cracks in the rocks. They stay there, often without eating or moving around much, until the weather warms up.

Deep mud gives this frog a cozy, warm winter home.

Yawn! These red-sided garter snakes are just waking up after their winter sleep.

The water-holding frog of Australia takes in large amounts of water through its skin and stores it in its body. When conditions are dry, the frog makes itself a watertight sack in the sand.

When summer gets too hot or too dry, many of these animals try to escape the heat. Some animals rest in the shade during the hot days and come out to hunt at night.

Others stay underground for weeks or months, until the cool weather returns. As in the winter, they are less active and don't eat much.

The desert tortoise burrows from a few inches to several feet underground.

# Use your SMART WORDS

Match each description with the correct Smart Word.

| adaptation | venom | predator |
|---|---|---|
| prey | camouflage | |

1. the poison produced by an animal

2. an animal that hunts and eats other animals for food

3. the ability of an animal to blend into its surroundings because of its color

4. a change that an animal goes through so it survives better in its habitat

5. an animal that is hunted and eaten by other animals

Answers on page 32

# Talk Like a Scientist

Write a paragraph for a tourist guidebook describing how to spot reptiles and amphibians in the wild. Explain why they might be difficult to see and how this is important for them. Use your Smart Words in your writing.

# SMART FACTS

## Did You Know?

The Komodo dragon is the largest living lizard. Males can grow up to 10 feet (3 meters) long and weigh almost 300 pounds (136 kilograms)!

## Good to Know

Komodo dragons are very patient. They use camouflage to hide until an animal comes by. Then they spring on the prey and gobble it up!

## That's Amazing!

Komodo dragons produce strong venom that kills the animals they bite. But when komodo dragons have fights and bite one another, the venom does not harm them.

# Glossary

**adaptation** a change that an animal goes through so it survives better in its habitat

**amphibian** an ectothermic vertebrate that lays eggs in water and usually has smooth, slimy skin

**burrow** to dig a hole or tunnel into the soil

**camouflage** the ability of an animal to blend into its surroundings because of its coloring

**classify** to arrange animals into groups according to how they are alike and different

**ectotherm** an animal whose body temperature depends on its surroundings

**egg** an oval or round structure that holds a young animal and the food it needs to develop

**gills** body structures that act like filters to move oxygen from the water into the body of an animal living in the water

**life cycle** the changes an animal goes through from the time it is born until it can produce young

**lungs** balloon-like structures that move oxygen from the air into the bodies of most animals that live on land

**metamorphosis** part of the life cycle during which an animal's body changes in form

**moist** damp or slightly wet

**predator** an animal that hunts and eats other animals for food

**prey** an animal that is hunted and eaten by other animals

**reptile** an animal that has a backbone, breathes air, has scaly skin, depends on its surroundings to maintain its body temperature, and may lay eggs or give live birth

**scales** thin, flat, overlapping pieces of hard skin that cover the bodies of most reptiles

**species** the most specific grouping of animals that share similar traits and can produce young

**temperature** a measure of how hot or cold something is

**venom** poison produced by an animal

**vertebrate** an animal with a backbone

# Index

# SMART WORDS Answer Key

**Page 10**
1. temperature, 2. reptile, 3. egg, 4. classify, 5. vertebrate,
6. ectotherm, 7. scales

**Page 20**
1. lungs, 2. metamorphosis, 3. burrow, 4. gills, 5. species,
6. amphibian, 7. moist, 8. life cycle

**Page 28**
1. venom, 2. predator, 3. camouflage, 4. adaptation, 5. prey